ABOUT THE BOOK

Crafted out of the love for the David's Psalms and Proverbs written by Solomon, I've written affirmations to deepen the spiritual bond with God the Father, the Son, and the Holy Spirit.

Turn the pages, read the words, and search the scriptures for additional affirmations that you can share with others.

You're encourage to wake up each morning and begin your day with The Word, The Truth, The Light, and The Way!

1

I HAVE BEEN MADE

I have been made in the image of God, not to be a stranger, but a ruler of a harmonious life.

Inspired by
Genesis 1:26

2
I FOLLOW

Abundance to come, I follow the commandments of God to fulfill the purpose of my existence.

Inspired by
Genesis 22:17

I ACCEPT MY NEW NAME

I accept my new name and emerge stronger, wiser, and transformed through God The Father and His Son Jesus Christ.

Inspired by
Genesis 32:28

4

I MAY QUESTION

I may question my abilities and purpose; however, I recognize that my worth and capabilities are not defined by my doubts.

Inspired by
Exodus 3:11

5

I AM A PECULIAR TREASURE

I am a peculiar treasure to God, above that which the world values.

Inspired by
Exodus 19:5

6

I LEARN TO REPENT

I learn to repent as The Lord taught and change my plans to align with God.

Inspired by
Exodus 32:14

I DO NOT FEAR TO CONFESS

I do not fear to confess the things that I have done to sin against God.

Inspired by
Leviticus 5:5

8

I RECOGNIZE THE VALUE

I recognize the value of life and the gift of atonement, to be cleaned by the blood of The Lamb of God.

Inspired by
Leviticus 17:11

9
I ACCEPT THE RAIN

My life is a garden of possibilities,
I accept the rain which God gives
in the seasons which He gives it.

Inspired by
Leviticus 26:4

10

I RELEASE MY STRESS

I release my stress and burdens, trusting that The Lord will illuminate my path forward to walk in the harmony of life.

Inspired by
Numbers 6:26

I REFLECT NOW AND ACCEPT

Through the cleansing waters of Christ, I reflect now and accept inner purification, allowing the divine waters to wash away my impurities.

Inspired by
Numbers 19:20

12

I HONOR MY COMMITMENTS

I honor my commitments and responsibilities, to myself and to those who The Lord has trusted after my care.

Inspired by
Numbers 30:15

13

I SEEK THE LORD

With all my heart and soul, I seek The Lord with unwavering devotion in my journey of discovery, hoping to find myself in the presence of The Lord.

Inspired by
Deuteronomy 4:29

I WILL BE VICTORIOUS

I will be victorious over my challenges and enemies, with a heart full of gratitude, the Lord will allow me rest.

Inspired by
Deuteronomy 25:19

15

I AM STRONG

I am strong and courageous, for The Lord is with me on this journey of life.

Inspired by
Joshua 1:6

16

I KNOW THE LORD WILL GIVE

I know The Lord will give all that
He promises to me, in due time I
shall receive what is mine.

Inspired by
Joshua 21:43

I AM LIKE A FIG TREE

I am like a fig tree, and I recognize the sweetness within myself, celebrating my uniqueness and valuable qualities.

Inspired by
Judges 9:11

18

I DRAW STRENGTH

As I face challenges and confrontations in life, I draw strength from The Lord who has provided for me always.

Inspired by
Judges 16:30

19

I RISE WITH DETERMINATION

I rise with determination and
resilience in the face of the day,
that I may be in the Lord's
presence who feeds all.

Inspired by
Ruth 1:6

20

I OPEN MY HEART

I open my heart to the riches of life's experiences and trust The Lord in the timing of my blessings.

Inspired by
Ruth 4:13

21

I MUST REMAIN MINDFUL

As I grow and evolve, I must remain mindful of the presence that I wish to accompany my journey, that I may grow aligned with God The Father.

Inspired by
1 Samuel 3:19

22

I PUT NO OTHER GOD BEFORE

In commitment to The Lord, I put no other God's before The Father whom all life was created, and all life is sustained.

Inspired by
1 Samuel 7:4

23
I HAVE NO NEED TO PERSUADE

I have no need to persuade, only listen to their words which speak their intentions and their hearts.

Inspired by
1 Samuel 20: 7

24

I EMBRACE ACCOUNTABILITY

I embrace accountability,
acknowledging the lessons
learned through my errors,
fearing not the words of truth.

Inspired by
2nd Samuel 12:7

25

I CAN FIND SOLACE

I will be reassured that in times of trouble I can find solace and strength in the sanctuary of God's love for me.

Inspired by
2nd Samuel 22:7

26

I RECOGNIZE THE IMPACT

Acknowledging my shortcomings and sins, I recognize the impact of my choices on those around me.

Inspired by
2nd Samuel 24:17

27
I SEEK FAIRNESS

I seek fairness and justice in the work of The Lord, that I may have insight to discern the truth with courage to do what is right.

Inspired by
1 Kings 3:27

28

I CANNOT DENY

I cannot deny who my God is, the God of Israel who is Jesus Christ and it is Him who I honor.

Inspired by
1 Kings 18:21

29

I AFFIRM MY TRUST

I affirm my trust in the divine guidance of The Holy Ghost who leads me to safe places.

Inspired by
2 Kings 1:15

30

I WILL NOT BE AFRAID

I will not be afraid for those who are with me are more than those who are against me, in all moments I am protected.

Inspired by
2nd Kings 6:16

31

I FIND THE SONG

I find the song of joyful service in the tabernacle, affirming my commitment to The Lord and all of Gods children.

Inspired by
1 Chronicles 6:32

I WILL DO IT FOR GOD

Whatever purpose or vision is in my heart, I will do it for God who is with me, moving forward knowing who The Lord is.

Inspired by
1 Chronicles 17:2

33

I LIFT MY PRAISE

With ears to hear and eyes to see, I lift my praise to The Lord, my God, recognizing the source of all blessings in life.

Inspired by
1 Chronicles 29:20

I HUMBLY ASK

I humbly ask for wisdom and knowledge to navigate the difficult path of being understood and to understand others.

Inspired by
2 Chronicles 1:10

35

I CHOOSE NOT TO GIVE UP

I choose not to give up, for my efforts may cause me to be weak, but my work will cause me to be rewarded by God.

Inspired by
2 Chronicles 15:7

36

I READY MYSELF

I ready myself to contribute positively to the lives of those around me by following the words of The Lord.

Inspired by
2 Chronicles 35:6

37

I COMMIT TO MAKE

Walking the spiritual path, I commit to make a continual offering of gratitude and devotion in my life and my actions may be a testament to my commitment.

Inspired by
Ezra 3:5

I KNOW A NEED

I know a need for repentance in the face of wrongdoing, like those who offered a ram for their guilt, I offer my sincere words and tears.

Inspired by
Ezra 10:19

39
I DELIGHT NO MORE

I delight no more in darkness,
asking that you hear my prayers,
that I may prosper in light this
day with mercy as my cup.

Inspired by
Nehemiah 1:11

40

I EMBRACE THE CONSEQUENCES

Standing firm in my convictions and principles, I embrace the consequences of the world which does not serve God.

Inspired by
Esther 3:5

41

I FEEL RESPONSIBLE

I feel responsible for the well-being of my people and seek to make a positive impact on their lives.

Inspired by
Esther 8:6

42

I AM HELD

I am held in the hands of The Lord and no trial shall take my eyes off the sights of Gods Kingdom.

Inspired by
Job 1:12

43

I AM A BEACON OF JUSTICE

Letting no wickedness dwell in the tabernacle of my soul, I am a beacon of justice, and my actions align with goodness.

Inspired by
Job 11:14

44

I CAN TRUST THE LORD

In the midst of life's trials, I can trust The Lord knows my path and will allow me to be made like gold.

Inspired by
Job 23:10

45

I NAVIGATE MY JOURNEY

With discernment, I navigate my journey walking with the positive influences and taking counsel from those who trust God.

Inspired by
Psalm 1:1

46

I EXTEND MY HAND

I extend my hand in mindfulness and may my actions reflect my understanding.

Inspired by
Psalm 8:4

47

I MUST COMMUNICATE

I must communicate with honesty, humility, and integrity, for God will silence the flattering lips and boastful tongue.

Inspired by
Psalm 12:3

48

I SEEK PROTECTION

I seek protection from The Lord, who will keep me from the harm of this world which seeks to devour those like me.

Inspired by
Psalm 17:14

49
I ACCEPTED THE PAIN

In agony my voice shakes and yet truth is known, I accepted the pain so that I may remain unshaken in the eternities.

Inspired by
Psalm 22:1

50

I JOIN IN PROCLAIMING

I join in proclaiming that Jesus Christ is The Almighty I Am who suffered and died and was risen for sinners like me.

Inspired by
Psalm 22:31

I FEAR NO EVIL

I fear no evil, for The Lord is
with me in the valley of death
and the peaks of life.

Inspired by
Psalm 23:4

52

I WAIT WITH HOPE

I wait with hope that I may be filled with the goodness of The King of Kings who strengthens my heart.

Inspired by
Psalm 27:14

I HAVE SINNED

I have sinned and now withhold nothing from The Lord, choosing not to cover up my transgression, I confess and receive forgiveness.

Inspired by
Psalm 32:5

54

I KNOW WHERE MY GOD IS

Though adversaries may taunt and question, I know where my God is, who is within me even as they mock me.

Inspired by
Psalm 42:10

55

I CHOOSE TO INVEST

I choose to invest my time and energy in the pursuits that have eternal significance and go beyond the boundaries of this life.

Inspired by
Psalm 49:17

56

I EXPRESS MY GRATITUDE

I express my gratitude for the salvation that God provides, which is through Jesus Christ whom I seek.

Inspired by
Psalm 70:4

I WILL CHOOSE A LIFE

I will choose a life dwelling in the house of The Lord as a servant over the master of a tent of wickedness.

Inspired by
Psalm 84:10

58

I TRUST

I trust The Lords guardianship over my life and declare that I hate evil, that evil which tries to bind mankind unto death.

Inspired by
Psalm 97:10

59

I MAKE

My life shall be an example, I make The Lords deeds known so that others can know his greatness.

Inspired by
Psalm 105:1

60

I PRACTICE A FEAR

I practice a fear which is love for The Lord, opening myself to wisdom and insight that reflects His ways.

Inspired by
Psalm 111:10

I CELEBRATE

I celebrate the craftmanship of my being, that God The Father has made me wonderfully, that my soul may know right.

Inspired by
Psalm 139:14

62

I AM RECEPTIVE

I am receptive to the instructions of wisdom, so that I can have understanding.

Inspired by
Proverbs 1:2

63

I REPRESENT MERCY

May these qualities be constant, I represent mercy and truth as if it were written on my heart.

Inspired by
Proverbs 3:3

I WAS A LIGHT

I was a light before I was born, and in that way an everlasting soul formed before the Earth and will live after the Earth is dead.

Inspired by
Proverbs 8:23

65

I TRUST PROSPERITY

I trust prosperity will follow my life as I give without expectation. The Lord will water me as I have watered others.

Inspired by
Proverbs 11:25

I MUST ALWAY CHOOSE

I must always choose the
path of wisdom and love,
for the alternative is anger
and wickedness.

Inspired by
Proverbs 14:17

67

I COMMIT TO BEING A FRIEND

I commit to being a friend at all times, loving and supportive to those who love and support God.

Inspired by
Proverbs 17:17

68

I AVOID THE PENALITIES

I avoid the penalties that come from evil by being willing to hide myself from those who demand a quick choice.

Inspired by
Proverbs 22:3

69

I DO NOT EAT

I do not eat with those who have an evil eye, nor desire what they have.

Inspired by
Proverbs 23:6

I STRIVE FOR BALANCE

In my life I strive for balance, neither vanity and lies, nor poverty or excess will satisfy my soul.

Inspired by
Proverbs 30:8

I LIVE IN HARMONY

I live in harmony knowing that each season of life is intended for me to find meaning and purpose, a time to be born and a time to die.

Inspired by
Ecclesiastes 3:2

I WILL BE AN INSTRUMENT

I will be an instrument of peace through the power of patience, which few poses and many die without knowing.

Inspired by
Ecclesiastes 7:9

I THEREFORE MUST CHERISH

Love is a force that cannot be quenched by many desires, I therefore must cherish and nurture the bonds that hold true significance.

Inspired by
Songs of Solomon 8:7

74

I SEEK AUTHENTIC CONNECTION

I seek authentic connection and genuine devotion as I give that which I seek, and The Lord accepts my heart.

Inspired by
Isaiah 1:13

I REJECT THOSE

I reject those who call evil good and good evil, putting away darkness by casing light and only partaking of The Lords sweet fruit.

Inspired by
Isaiah 5:20

I ACCEPT PURIFICATION

Embracing the transformative power of divine light, I accept purification through the fires of my life so that I may be clean before The Lord.

Inspired by
Isaiah 10:17

I PLACE TRUST AND NOT FEAR

I place trust and not fear in The Lord, He is salivation coming to my aid, and turning my weaknesses into strengths.

Inspired by
Isaiah 12:2

I AM GRATEFUL

In times of trouble there is refuge, I am grateful for the unwavering love of The Lord who is my strength.

Inspired by
Isaiah 25:4

79

I SEEK YOU

I seek you in the day and in the night, in the early hours and when judgement shall come.

Inspired by
Isaiah 26:9

I AM ASTOUNDED

I am astounded by the wonders
that unfold by The Word of God,
that can an unlearned person such
as me and allow me to be wise.

Inspired by
Isaiah 29:14

81

I THEN WILL SEE

May the love of God touch my eyes,
I then will see, and may His love
touch my ears that no words will
escape, or message will be missed.

Inspired by
Isaiah 35:5

I RISE ABOVE DIFFICULTIES

With trust in the divine, I rise above difficulties and soar higher as my strength is renewed in patience.

Inspired by
Isaiah 40:31

83

I FIND HOPE THAT HE IS

There is no other like Him, I find hope that He is the one true God, and His power is unmatched.

Inspired by
Isaiah 46:9

I SHAKE OFF MY DUST

I shake off my dust of limitations, rising to sit on the throne, freed from the chains that once had me bound.

Inspired by
Isaiah 52:2

I FORSAKE MY WAYS

I forsake my ways, now my thoughts return to The Lord who will have mercy on me, pardoning me now.

Inspired by
Isaiah 55:7

86

I WILL EMBODY

Arising today the light has come,
I will embody the risen Lord
who I will give glory to this day.

Inspired by
Isaiah 60:1

I AM THE WORK

I am the work of your hands, guide me, shape me, and transform me into a vessel that you can use today.

Inspired by
Isaiah 64:8

I AM COURAGEOUS KNOWING

I am courageous knowing that I do not fight alone, and nothing will prevail against me for The Lord does deliver me from evil.

Inspired by
Jeremiah 1:19

I AM OPEN TO CHANGE

In the spirit of repentance, I am open to change, turning away from the evil which I knew and toward the Light of The World.

Inspired by
Jeremiah 18:8

90

I AM FILLED WITH PEACE

As I wait upon The Lord, I am filled with peace and assurance that my portion is secure and my needs are met.

Inspired by
Lamentations 3:24

I CHOOSE TO ALIGN MYSELF

May my intentions be pure, and my eyes set on God, I choose to align myself with none other than The Lord Jesus Christ.

Inspired By
Ezekiel 14:3

I KNOW HIS WATCHFUL EYES

Confident that his justice prevails, I know His watchful eyes are over me and I find peace in that knowledge.

Inspired by
Ezekiel 34:22

93

I AM NOT A STRANGER

I am not a stranger, rather I now align my actions to the offering of the flesh and of the blood which has covenanted with me.

Inspired by
Ezekiel 44:7

I TRUST THE PROTECTION

Like those who faced the fiery furnace, I trust the protection of God as I remain devoted to His worship.

Inspired by
Daniel 3:6

95
I SET MY FACE TO THE LORD

I set my face to The Lord, praying that I may receive what will be sufficient for my needs and the needs of my loved ones.

Inspired by
Daniel 9:3

I ASPIRE TO BE AMONG

I aspire to be among the wise who shine like the brightness of the heavens, that I may turn many to righteousness.

Inspired by
Daniel 12:3

I FIND RESTORATION

I find restoration as I return to His loving presence, seeking the goodness that is God.

Inspired by
Hosea 3:5

98

I AM HIS CHILD

I am His child, drawn to his presence with reverence and awe, may His roar which causes others to tremble cause me to worship.

Inspired by
Hosea 11:10

99

I FORTIFY MY FAITH

Knowing His presence is near, I fortify my faith to embrace the spiritual call and avoid destruction of my soul.

Inspired by
Joel 1:15

I CONTRIBTUE TO THE WORK

May my words and actions be wise, I contribute to the work through silence, trusting in God and the plans He has for me.

Inspired by
Amos 5:13

101

I DO SO WITH REVERENCE

As a partake in the experiences of life, I do so with reverence and respect, not allowing unholy drinks to touch my lips nor unholy words come from my lips.

Inspired by
Obadiah 1:16

102

I SIMPLY NEED TO TRUST

Even in the midst of my difficulties The Lord is responsive, I simply need to trust that He hears my cries.

Inspired by
Jonah 2:2

103

I NAVIGATE LIFE'S JOURNEY

I navigate life's journey even as I stand and feed in the strength of The Lord, knowing my destiny is greatness.

Inspired by
Micah 5:4

I PUBLISH PEACE

I publish peace, bringing good tidings of The Lord, who is The Lion of Judah.

Inspired by
Nahum 1:15

105

I FIND A SACRED SPACE

I find a sacred space in
stillness, holding my tongue
before The Lord.

Inspired by
Habakkuk 2:20

I PATIENTLY AWAIT

I patiently await the fulfillment of His divine purposes, and in my heart aligning with His will and avoiding His anger.

Inspired by
Zephaniah 3:8

107

I GAIN INSIGHT

I gain insight into the joy that comes from progress as I sow the seeds and tend the fields of my life.

Inspired by
Haggai 2:19

I ONLY WISH

Abide with me Lord Jesus, I only wish to be among those whom you have found worthy among all nations.

Inspired by
Zechariah 2:11

109
I WILL NOT MOURN

I will not mourn, knowing my ways have turned from evil and toward The Lord, who died for my sins.

Inspired by
Zechariah 12:11

110

I HAVE SOUGHT YOU

Be gracious unto me Lord, I have sought you and stive to live in a way which honors and pleases you.

Inspired by
Malachi 1:9

I HOPE

Turning my heart now, I hope that all those whom I love will turn toward the Lord who will save them from the great curse.

Inspired by
Malachi 4:6

My aim in writing these affirmations was to create a space where readers could find inspiration, reflection, and a sense of spiritual connection. Your decision to explore these affirmations from The Old Testament means the world to me, and I hope they bring moments of peace, encouragement, and personal growth to your life as you journey on.

MATTHEW LUKE WEBSTER

Made in the USA
Columbia, SC
26 January 2024